THE
TOTALLY
CAMPING
COOKBOOK

D0451087

THE TOTALLY CAMPING COOKBOOK

by Helene Siegel

CELESTIAL ARTS
BERKELEY, CALIFORNIA

The Totally Camping Cookbook is produced by becker&mayer!, Ltd.

Printed in Singapore.

Cover design and illustration: Bob Greisen
Interior design and typesetting: Susan Hernday
Interior illustrations: Carolyn Vibbert

Library of Congress Cataloging-in-Publication Data
Siegel, Helene.
Totally Camping / by Helene Siegel
    p.   cm.
ISBN 0-89087-807-2
1.Outdoor cookery.   I. Title.
TX823.S458   1996
641.5'78—dc20   96-24084
                  CIP

Celestial Arts Publishing
P.O. Box 7123
Berkeley, CA 94707

Other cookbooks in this series:
The Totally Burgers Cookbook
The Totally Chocolate Cookbook
The Totally Pancakes & Waffles Cookbook

Thanks to the Weavers—
Jay, Paula, Ben and Adam
—good campers and friends.

TABLE
OF
CONTENTS

INTRODUCTION

Let's get our priorities straight. This is a book for those who care more about what they eat than how they can pack the most efficient backpack or how to air-drop a parcel of food onto the tundra. Other more rugged individuals have tackled those subjects with greater authority.

When it comes to outdoor cooking, good taste has played second fiddle to strange priorities for long enough. Who really wants to eat foods named gorp, pemmican, or jerky—or a dehydrated slice of pizza or ice cream packaged in tin foil? It seems to me that when Americans set out for a weekend of sleeping under the stars, they should reward themselves with naturally delicious real foods that are as good as anything they would eat at home. Eating well on a camping trip need not be complicated.

The model for the recipes included herein is a family of four setting out for a weekend of car camping. They should have an ice chest for perishables, a two-burner camp stove (with three small cans of fuel if they're using propane), a grate to throw over a campfire for an instant grill, a 10-inch nonstick skillet, and a standard cookware set of two or three pots (with lids) in graduated sizes. A portable camp oven for placing over the stovetop is desirable but optional, and a backpack or two for day hikes is de rigueur.

Since there are better things to do outside than putter around a makeshift kitchen or clean up, all of these meals are easy to prepare: lots of marinades and grills, easy pasta sauces with a method for preboiling the pasta at home, foil packet–baked chicken and fish specialties, one-pot suppers, and a few spice rubs, hot drinks, and fruit desserts—not to mention variations on the classic s'mores theme.

All are good enough to eat at home, but under the stars or on a crisp cool morning, they will taste much better.

BREAKFAST
FIXINGS

HOMEMADE GRANOLA

The beauty of making your own granola is the ability it gives you to tailor the sugar and other flavors to taste. This lightly sweetened version is chock-full of nuts. Keep a supply at home and pack in zipper-lock bags for taking along.

2 cups rolled oats
¼ cup wheat germ
¾ cup whole almonds with skins, roughly
    chopped
½ teaspoon cinnamon
¼ teaspoon ground nutmeg
⅓ cup vegetable or safflower oil
3 tablespoons honey
2 tablespoons maple syrup
1 tablespoon grated orange zest
½ cup golden raisins
½ cup chopped dried apple slices

Preheat oven to 325 degrees F.

In large bowl, combine oats, wheat germ, almonds, cinnamon, and nutmeg.

Combine oil, honey, maple syrup, and orange zest in small pot. Cook over low heat to warm through. Pour over oat mixture, stirring well to coat evenly.

Transfer to baking sheet and bake 30 minutes, stirring once or twice to brown evenly. Let cool and transfer to bowl. Stir in raisins and apples. Store in sealed container.

MAKES 5 CUPS, 10 SERVINGS

HOT POLENTA WITH APRICOTS AND PINE NUTS

Try substituting chopped pecans or walnuts, raisins, and maple syrup in your instant cornmeal mush.

2 cups water
salt
1 cup instant polenta
¼ cup brown sugar
½ cup chopped dried apricots
2 tablespoons butter or margarine
½ cup pine nuts

Bring salted water to a boil. Add polenta, sugar, and apricots. Cook, stirring frequently, about 5 minutes, until water is absorbed. Stir in butter and nuts until melted and serve hot in cups or bowls.

SERVES 6

INSTANT
HUEVOS RANCHEROS

In case you were wondering what to do with that half-eaten bag of chips in the car, try this delicious instant Mexican breakfast or light supper.

1 cup prepared tomato salsa
1½ cups half-and-half
½ (13-ounce) bag tortilla chips (about 4 cups)
½ cup shredded cheddar cheese
1 tablespoon butter or margarine
4 eggs

Combine the salsa and half-and-half in saucepan. Bring to a boil. Stir in chips, crushing with spoon. Reduce to simmer and cook until chips soften, forming a mush. Stir in cheese and remove from heat.

Melt butter in nonstick skillet over high heat. Fry eggs, sunny-side up or over easy. Transfer chip mixture to bowls and top each with an egg.

SERVES 4

HOT POLENTA WITH CHILES AND CORN

Another instant cornmeal mush—this time flavored with sweet corn and roasted chiles.

2 cups water
salt
1 cup instant polenta
1 (7-ounce) can corn kernels, drained
3 tablespoons canned diced, roasted green chiles
1 cup shredded cheddar cheese
prepared salsa (optional)

Bring salted water to a boil. Stir in polenta and cook until water is absorbed, a few minutes. Stir in corn, chiles, and cheese. Spoon into bowls and top with dollop of salsa, if desired.

SERVES 6

HOT OATMEAL WITH ADDITIONS

Other great additions to plain oatmeal: raisins, maple syrup, "Sweet Spice Mix" (see page 23), bananas, chopped dried apricots, or apples.

    instant oatmeal
    boiling water
    trail mix with chocolate chips and raisins

Place oatmeal in bowls and pour ½ cup boiling water over each serving. Stir to moisten evenly, sprinkle in trail mix, and stir some more.

MUFFIN CAKES L'ORANGE

*Chef Mary Sue Milliken remembers these from
early childhood campouts. You may want to do
them at night since they do take some time to
bake. They are spectacular for breakfast, drizzled
with maple syrup.*

4 large oranges, washed
1 cup Bisquick
1 tablespoon sugar
½ cup milk
maple syrup for drizzling (optional)

Start the camp fire. Trim the top
¼-inch off oranges and reserve. Using
a serrated grapefruit knife or spoon,
remove pulp and membranes from orange.
Eat fruit and drink juice from hollowed-out
orange peel cup.

In a bowl, mix together Bisquick, sugar, and
milk. Spoon batter into hollowed oranges,
halfway to the top. Cover each with reserved
top and tightly wrap with foil to seal. Bury in
hot coals or bake in reflector oven until set,
about 1 hour. Unwrap, let cool, and eat with a
spoon. Drizzle with maple syrup if desired.

SERVES 4

PB&J FRENCH TOAST

What I imagine Elvis would eat for breakfast if he ever spent the night on the ground—gooey, messy, rich peanut butter toast, dripping with maple syrup.

wheat bread
peanut butter
strawberry or raspberry jelly
eggs
milk
butter or margarine
maple syrup for drizzling

For each serving, make a peanut butter and jelly sandwich, spreading the fillings thinly.

In a shallow container or pan, whisk the eggs (1 per sandwich) with 1 tablespoon or so of milk. Dip the sandwiches and soak 5 minutes, turning once to coat evenly.

Melt 2 tablespoons of butter in large skillet over medium heat. Fry the sandwiches until golden brown on both sides. Serve hot with maple syrup.

GRILLED CHEESE AND BACON

Grilled sandwiches with bacon make a good, hearty breakfast for a cold morning.

16 slices wheat or white bread
1 pound sliced cheddar, American, or
    Monterey Jack cheese
8 bacon slices, fried, and drained
softened butter or margarine

Butter all the bread on one side. Layer cheese on uncoated side of 8 bread slices. Break bacon in half and place over cheese. Close sandwiches with remaining slices, buttered-side up.

Melt a tablespoon of butter in a large skillet over medium heat. Fry the sandwiches, a few at a time, until bottoms are golden and crisp. (Reduce heat if bread is blackening.) Turn and briefly cook second side until bread is golden and cheese is melted.

MAKES 8

SWEET SPICE MIX

½ cup brown sugar
1 teaspoon cinnamon
½ teaspoon ground nutmeg
pinch of salt
¼ cup raisins
½ cup unsweetened grated coconut

Mix together in bowl, breaking up sugar lumps with fork. Store in zipper-lock bag. Sprinkle on hot oatmeal, plain yogurt, toast, and pancakes.

MAKES ¾ CUP

HOT
DRINKS

CAMPFIRE COFFEE

whole coffee beans

At home, grind the beans and store in zipper-lock bag or plastic container.

At campsite, on stovetop, bring water to boil. Place 1 tablespoon of coffee for each serving in a paper coffee filter with holder and pour hot water through grounds into cups or thermos.

HOT MOCHA

chocolate syrup
freshly brewed strong coffee
warm milk
marshmallows

Pour 1 teaspoon chocolate syrup in each cup. Fill with two-thirds coffee and one-third milk. Stir, top with a marshmallow, and drink.

SPICED APPLE JUICE

2 cups apple juice
8 whole cloves
2 cinnamon sticks
1 lemon

Combine the juice, cloves, and cinnamon in a small pot. Cut the lemon in half, squeeze, and add to pot. Cook over medium heat until nearly to a boil. Remove and let steep 5 minutes. Strain and serve with cinnamon sticks.

SERVES 2

HOT CHAI

3 tablespoons black breakfast tea
¼ cup brown sugar
6 whole cloves
2 cinnamon sticks
½ cup milk or half-and-half
3 cups water
4 cinnamon sticks for serving

Combine all the ingredients in a small pot. Bring to a simmer and cook 5 minutes. Remove from heat and let steep 10 minutes. Strain into mugs and serve with cinnamon sticks.

SERVES 4

HOT POTS
AND
SKILLET SUPPERS

PASTA WITH SAUSAGE AND TOMATOES

Nothing beats pasta and meat when it comes to filling empty stomachs until morning. In all of the pasta recipes, the pasta can either be prepared at home or cooked at the site—just bring along a strainer and remember to allow time for boiling a large pot of water.

1 pound pasta
5 tablespoons olive oil
1 medium onion, chopped
4 turkey sausages, cut in ½-inch lengths
1 (28-ounce) can crushed tomatoes
1 tablespoon dried crushed oregano
salt and pepper to taste
grated Parmesan cheese for sprinkling

At home, cook the pasta in salted water. Drain, rinse with cold water and transfer to large bowl. Add 3 tablespoons of oil, toss to coat evenly and transfer to large zipper-lock bag. Store in ice chest.

At campsite, remove pasta from cooler to warm to ambient temperature. Heat 2 tablespoons oil in large nonstick skillet over medium heat. Sauté onions until starting to soften. Add sausage and fry until evenly browned. Add tomatoes, oregano, salt, and pepper. Simmer until thickened to taste, about 15 minutes.

Add pasta to sauce to heat through. If pan is too small, place pasta in serving bowl, top with hot sauce, and toss well. Serve hot with Parmesan for sprinkling.

SERVES 4

GREEN-AND-WHITE VEGETARIAN PASTA

Here is a pretty, healthful, white-and-green pasta made with two favorite inexpensive, easy-to-find vegetables—broccoli and cauliflower.

1 pound corkscrew or fusilli pasta
½ cup olive oil
8 garlic cloves, minced
2 stalks broccoli florets, blanched
½ head cauliflower florets, blanched
½ teaspoon red pepper flakes
lemon juice
salt and pepper
grated Parmesan for sprinkling

At home, cook the pasta in salted water. Drain, rinse with cold water, and transfer to large bowl. Add 3 tablespoons of oil, toss to coat evenly and transfer to large zipper-lock bag. Pack blanched broccoli and cauliflower in another zipper-lock bag. Store in ice chest.

At campsite, remove pasta from cooler and warm to ambient temperature. Heat remaining oil in large skillet over medium-high heat. Cook garlic until golden. Add broccoli, cauliflower, red pepper, lemon juice, salt, and pepper, and cook over low heat until soft, about 15 minutes.

Add pasta to sauce to heat through or if pan is too small, place pasta in serving bowl. Top with hot sauce and toss well. Serve hot with Parmesan for sprinkling.

SERVES 4

CHICKEN AND HAM JAMBALAYA

With apologies to the Cajun master Paul Prudhomme, here is an easy take on his rib-sticking standard. Serve with a mixed green salad.

2 tablespoons vegetable oil
1 (6-ounce) slice honey-baked ham,
    cut in chunks
1 skinless, boneless chicken breast half,
    cut in chunks
3 teaspoons "Cajun Spice Mix" (see page 94)
2 garlic cloves, minced
½ large onion, chopped
1 green bell pepper, seeded and chopped
1 cup prepared tomato sauce
1 cup converted rice
2 cups water
salt and pepper

Heat oil in large nonstick skillet over high heat. Sauté ham until beginning to brown. Add chicken and sauté until brown. Stir in spice mix, garlic, onion, and peppers, and cook over medium heat until softened. Add tomato sauce, cook 1 minute, and add rice and water. Stir well, reduce to simmer and cover tightly. Cook until liquid is absorbed and rice is done, about $\frac{1}{2}$ hour. Adjust seasonings with salt and pepper and serve hot in bowls.

SERVES 2 TO 4

BUCKWHEAT GROATS AND NOODLES

This Russian Jewish favorite, kasha varnishkes, is usually served as a side dish, but it makes an exceptionally delicious, nourishing, inexpensive meal for cool-weather camping.

1 egg
1 cup buckwheat groats
2 tablespoons butter or margarine
2 cups boiling water
1 onion, chopped
2 garlic cloves, minced
1 (7-ounce) package bowtie egg noodles
salt and pepper

Lightly beat egg in mixing bowl.
Add buckwheat and stir with fork to
coat evenly.

Melt 1 tablespoon of butter in large skillet
over high heat. Add buckwheat and cook, stirring frequently, until grains are dry and sepa-
rate. Pour in hot water, cover, and simmer
until water is absorbed, about 20 minutes.

Meanwhile, in small pan, melt remaining
butter over medium-high heat. Sauté onion
with garlic until golden. Reserve.

Cook noodles in boiling salted water. Drain.

When groats are done, stir in onion mixture and noodles. Season to taste with salt and
pepper, and serve hot.

SERVES 4

SALAMI AND EGG FRIED RICE

Use leftover rice from yesterday's dinner for this hearty breakfast or dinner.

3 cups cooked, cooled rice
¼ cup vegetable or peanut oil
1 onion, chopped
4 ounces salami, peeled and
    cut in ¼-inch chunks
2 eggs, beaten
soy sauce
Tabasco sauce
sesame oil (optional)
salt and pepper to taste

At home, cook the rice and store in zipper-lock bag or plastic container. Store in ice chest.

At campsite, heat half the oil in a large nonstick skillet over high heat. Sauté onion until golden. Add salami and fry briefly, until edges are brown. Remove from pan and reserve.

Add remaining oil to pan and add rice. Fry until golden and crisp and transfer to bowl. Pour eggs into hot pan and scramble. Return onion salami mixture and rice to pan and stir-fry to combine and heat through. Season to taste with soy, Tabasco, sesame oil (if desired), salt, and pepper. Serve hot in bowls.

SERVES 4

COUSCOUS SALAD WITH ROASTED PEPPERS

1 cup instant couscous
1 cup water
1 garlic clove, crushed
2 tablespoons olive oil
juice of 1 lemon
2 red, yellow, or orange bell peppers
1 small red onion
2 tablespoons chopped fresh basil
½ cup crumbled feta cheese
salt and pepper

At home, place couscous in mixing bowl.

Combine the water, garlic, and oil in small saucepan and bring to a boil. Pour over the couscous and cover. Let sit 15 minutes. Sprinkle with lemon juice, fluff with a fork, and remove garlic. Add remaining ingredients, mix well, and season to taste with salt and pepper. Store in plastic container, and chill or pack in ice chest.

SERVES 4 TO 6

TURKEY WHITE BEAN CHILI

If you don't want to take along individual spices, substitute "Mexican Spice Mix" (see page 42).

3 tablespoons vegetable oil
1½ onions, chopped
3 garlic cloves, minced
1 serrano or jalapeño chile,
    chopped with seeds
1½ pounds ground turkey
2 teaspoons ground cumin
½ teaspoon ground coriander
1 tablespoon dried parsley or oregano
salt and pepper
2 tomatoes, chopped
1 (15-ounce) can white beans, drained
juice of 1 lemon or 2 limes
tortillas

Heat the olive oil in a large skillet over medium heat. Cook the onions until soft, add the garlic and chile pepper, and cook briefly, just until the aroma is released.

Push the onions to the edges and add turkey, cumin, coriander, dried parsley or oregano, salt, and pepper to the center of the pan. Turn up the heat and cook, breaking up the meat with a spoon, stirring and tossing to coat evenly. Stir in the tomatoes. Reduce the heat and cook, uncovered, until the pan is nearly dry. Stir in the beans and lemon juice and cook just to heat through, 5 to 10 minutes. Serve hot in bowls with warm tortillas.

SERVES 4

INSTANT
TOMATO SALMON SAUCE
FOR PASTA

This easy pasta sauce from a can was inspired by Marcella Hazan's "Tuna and Tomato Sauce" from her first book.

1 pound spaghetti
3 tablespoons olive oil
2 garlic cloves, minced
¾ (28-ounce) can Italian crushed tomatoes
salt and freshly ground pepper
1 (7.5-ounce) can red salmon
½ bunch chopped fresh basil leaves
juice of 1 lemon

At home, cook the pasta in salted water. Drain, rinse with cold water, and transfer to large bowl. Add 1 tablespoon of oil, toss to coat evenly and transfer to large zipper-lock bag. Store in ice chest.

At the campsite, heat 2 tablespoons of the oil in a large skillet over medium heat. Cook the garlic to soften. Add the tomatoes, season with salt and pepper, and cook over low heat, stirring occasionally, until thickened to a sauce.

Open the can of salmon, remove skin and bone, and flake meat with a fork. Stir into the tomato sauce, along with the basil, and cook to heat through, 5 to 10 minutes. Season with lemon juice and salt and pepper. Add the pasta and toss to coat or transfer to serving bowl, along with pasta, and toss well.

SERVES 4

HUNGARIAN HOT DOGS IN THE SKILLET

Lecso is a traditional Hungarian appetizer of onions, peppers, and hot dogs.

2 tablespoons vegetable oil
1 medium onion, sliced
2 large green bell peppers, cored, seeded, and sliced
1 (14.5-ounce) can chopped tomatoes
salt, pepper, and sugar to taste
1 tablespoon paprika
4 hot dogs, cut in 1-inch lengths

Heat the oil in a large skillet over medium-high heat. Sauté the onion until beginning to soften. Add the peppers and cook, stirring frequently, until softened.

Stir in the tomatoes, sugar, salt, pepper, paprika, and hot dogs. Reduce heat to low and cook, uncovered, about 10 minutes. Serve hot in bowls.

SERVES 4

JULIE'S BEAN THING

Serve this instant vegetarian chili in a bowl or rolled in a flour tortilla like a burrito, and dress it up with sour cream or plain yogurt and a few other garnishes as suggested.

2 tablespoons olive oil
1 medium onion, chopped
2 celery ribs, diced
1 garlic clove, minced
½ to 1 teaspoon red chile flakes
1 (15-ounce) can chopped tomatoes
2 (15-ounce) cans black beans, drained
salt and pepper
juice of 1 lemon
tortillas, chopped fresh cilantro,
    shredded Jack or cheddar cheese

Heat the oil in a large skillet over medium heat. Sauté the onion and celery until soft and golden. Add the garlic and chile flakes, turn up the heat, and cook a few minutes to release their flavor.

Add the tomatoes and black beans and cook, stirring occasionally, about 10 to 15 minutes. Season with salt and pepper and serve with tortillas and suggested garnishes.

SERVES 4

PAN-FRIED TROUT
WITH ALMONDS

If you do catch your own fish, place it on ice after gutting and let it rest until rigor mortis leaves the body in an hour or two. Fish that is cooked too soon has an unpleasant, mushy texture.

¼ cup all-purpose flour
¼ cup ground almonds
½ teaspoon paprika
2 whole trout, gutted and scaled
salt and pepper
butter or margarine
lemons for garnish

At home mix together the flour, almonds, and paprika. Store in zipper-lock bag or long, shallow plastic container.

At the campsite, salt and pepper the fish inside and out. Dip into the flour mixture or pat on to coat evenly. Heat a cast-iron or non-stick skillet over high heat. Melt a tablespoon of so of butter to thinly coat the pan.

Fry the fish 1 or 2 minutes to sear both sides. Then reduce the heat to medium-low and continue cooking, flipping frequently, until cooked through (check the inside for doneness), about 8 minutes longer. Sprinkle with lemon juice and serve with lemon wedges.

SERVES 2

Quick Getaways

Rather than purchase brand-new equipment for cooking outdoors, I like to recycle old favorites and keep them in the "camp-out corner" of the garage for instant summer getaways. Old pots and pans, slightly split cutting boards, silverware that has been chewed on by the garbage disposal, and battered old knives all get placed in a special corner, along with other accouterments such as camp stove and bug repellent.

TOTALLY GRILLED DINNERS

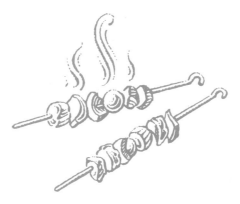

ITALIAN
GRILLED DINNER

Round out this lovely, healthful Italian meal with a loaf of crusty bread for grilling, olive oil for drizzling on the bread and premixed salad, and vinegar or lemons for the salad. For dessert, pack some hard, dry biscotti—easy to transport and always delicious.

LEMON ROSEMARY CHICKEN

4 to 8 skinless, boneless chicken breasts
1 cup olive oil
½ cup lemon juice
6 garlic cloves, chopped
3 tablespoons dried rosemary or 3 large sprigs
    chopped fresh rosemary leaves
salt and freshly ground pepper

At home, pound the chicken breasts to flatten.
In a bowl, whisk together oil, lemon juice,
garlic, rosemary, and generous amounts of salt
and pepper. Place chicken in large zipper-lock
bag, add marinade, press out air, and seal.
Pack in ice chest.

At campsite, preheat grill or start fire.
Remove chicken, shake off excess marinade,
and grill about 10 minutes per side.

SERVES 4 TO 6

GRILLED VEGETABLES

Since summer vegetables are quite perishable, purchase vegetables, if possible, close to your campsite. If you are bringing from home, do not precut or store on ice. They will keep best in a brown paper bag tossed into the trunk of the car.

red peppers, seeded and quartered
zucchinis, trimmed and quartered lengthwise
Japanese eggplant with skin, trimmed and
    sliced lengthwise
olive oil or garlic-infused oil
balsamic vinegar or lemon wedges (optional)
    garnish

Lightly coat vegetables with oil. Alongside or after the chicken, grill vegetables over indirect flames until lightly charred, turning several times. Drizzle with vinegar or lemon juice, if desired, and serve alongside chicken.

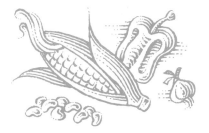

Ingredients to Go

Store butter in the ice chest in a sealed plastic container. Purchase milk in plastic containers and store eggs in the specially designed plastic containers available at camping stores. Buy individually packed instant oatmeals and hot chocolate for convenience.

For instant minced garlic, process a head or two of peeled cloves in the food processor or blender with a bit of olive oil. Transfer to a small plastic sealable container. Minced garlic is also available in jars at the market.

CHINESE
GRILLED DINNER

All you need to accompany this quick grilled dinner is rice or tortillas (similar enough to Chinese pancakes to do in a pinch), beer, and a good bag of cookies for dessert. Or if you are feeling more ambitious, cut some oranges into thick slices and lightly grill after the coals have cooled slightly.

SOY PORK CHOPS

¼ cup soy sauce
¼ cup dry sherry
2 tablespoons hoisin sauce
1 tablespoon minced garlic
1 tablespoon minced ginger
3 scallions, sliced
½ to 1 pound wafer-thin pork chops
Thai peanut sauce (optional) for dipping

At home, whisk together soy sauce, sherry,
hoisin sauce, garlic, ginger, and scallions.
Place pork chops in zipper-lock bag, pour on
marinade, and seal, pressing out air. Pack in
ice chest.

At campsite, prepare grill. Remove from
marinade and grill pork until meat is white
and lightly charred on both sides. Serve hot
with dipping sauce, if desired.

SERVES 2 TO 4

GRILLED ASPARAGUS

16 asparagus spears, ends trimmed
3 tablespoons peanut oil
1 tablespoon sesame oil
2 teaspoons honey
1 tablespoon soy sauce
2 tablespoons rice wine vinegar
3 garlic cloves, minced
salt and pepper to taste

At home, blanch asparagus spears in salted water or in microwave at high power for 2 minutes. Drain and place in plastic container or bag.

In small bowl, whisk together remaining ingredients. Pour over asparagus, seal, and pack in ice chest or chill.

At campsite, prepare grill. Grill briefly, over low flames, turning frequently, until lightly and evenly charred. Season with salt and pepper and serve hot.

SERVES 4

The Right Stuff

Though I love good, solid kitchen equipment, when it comes to cooking outside, common sense and good economy must prevail. Everything ages quickly in the great outdoors. Rather than sacrifice an exquisite new skillet, take along inexpensive aluminum pots and pans, extra steak knives, or an extra nonstick pan picked up at a flea market or discount store.

THAI
GRILLED DINNER

Marinated chicken on skewers with its traditional Thai accompaniments—sweet and spicy cucumber salad and peanut sauce— is a snap. Just boil some rice and bring along more peanut sauce than you think you'll need—it makes a nice spicy dip for cut-up vegetables and fruit and a dressing for salad.

CHICKEN SATAY

¼ cup white wine
¼ cup fish or soy sauce
1 tablespoon peanut oil
2 tablespoons lime or lemon juice
3 garlic cloves, chopped
4 skinless, boneless chicken breast halves,
    cut in strips
prepared Thai peanut sauce

At home, whisk together wine, fish sauce, oil, lime juice, and garlic. Place chicken strips in zipper-lock bag, pour on marinade, and seal, pressing out air. Pack in ice chest along with skewers.

At campsite, prepare the grill. Remove chicken strips from marinade and thread each on skewer. Grill until meat is opaque and lightly charred all over, turning frequently to avoid burning. Serve with peanut sauce for dipping.

SERVES 4

CUCUMBER SALAD

¼ cup sugar
1 teaspoon salt
⅛ teaspoon red pepper flakes
½ cup rice vinegar
3 medium cucumbers, peeled, quartered
    lengthwise, seeded, and sliced
¼ red onion, finely diced

At home, combine sugar, salt, red pepper, and rice vinegar in small saucepan. Bring to boil, reduce to simmer, and cook until clear, about 5 minutes. Let cool.

Place cucumbers and onion in plastic container. Pour on vinegar mixture and toss to coat evenly. Chill or pack in ice chest.

SERVES 4

Must Haves
can opener
garbage bags
zipper-lock bags
small bottle liquid soap for dishes
sponges
paper towels
corkscrew
freshly ground coffee packed in zipper-lock bags
    and coffee filters

MEXICAN GRILLED DINNER

Mexican food always feels festive, especially when you remember the beer and lime wedges. Tortillas can be stacked, wrapped in foil, and kept warm and pliable on a cooler spot of the grill. While the grill is heating, open a bag of tortilla chips with prepared salsa or bean dip for nibbling.

CITRUS-MARINATED CHICKEN TACOS

½ cup orange juice
2 canned chipotle chiles
1 tablespoon lime or lemon juice
1 cup prepared tomato salsa
2 tablespoons vegetable oil
salt and pepper to taste
4 to 6 skinless, boneless chicken breast halves
tortillas
additional salsa and chopped onion for garnish

At home, combine orange juice, chipotles, lime or lemon juice, salsa, oil, salt, and pepper in blender or food processor. Purée. Place chicken breasts in large zipper-lock bag, pour on marinade, and seal, pressing out air.

At campsite, prepare grill. Remove chicken from marinade and grill, turning frequently to prevent burns, until done, about 15 minutes total. Stack tortillas and wrap in foil. Warm on grill about 10 minutes in cool spot. Chop chicken into bite-size pieces and serve wrapped in warm tortillas with salsa and onion as garnish.

SERVES 4 TO 6

GRILLED CORN AND ZUCCHINI

zucchinis, halved lengthwise
vegetable oil
ears of corn, with silks and husks
butter or margarine
chile powder
salt and pepper
lime wedges

Prepare grill. Brush zucchinis with oil.

Grill corn in husks until evenly charred, about 20 minutes. Remove from grill and using a towel to protect your hands, fold back husks and silk. Return to grill and cook 7 minutes longer, turning frequently.

Grill zucchinis until evenly charred and softened.

Brush both with butter or margarine and season with chile, salt, and pepper. Sprinkle with lime juice and serve corn with husks for holding

Ingredients to Go

Purchase small, portable containers of staples such as mayonnaise, ketchup, olive oil, vinegar, salt, and pepper. Margarine and Bisquick are available in small squeeze bottles at the supermarket. Check out the picnic section for more ideas.

If you love Italian flavors, transfer olive oil to a plastic picnic squeeze bottle for easy access for grilling and salad dressings.

Either purchase grated cheese or grate at home and pack in zipper-lock bags.

MOCK
TANDOORI CHICKEN

Indian-style tandoori chicken has a delightful fruity aroma and bright orange color. If you are near a market, bring along puffed pappadams or grill flat bread for a nice smoky flavor. Serve with rice, fruit, and prepared mango chutney.

½ onion, in large chunks
1 tablespoon minced fresh ginger
1 tablespoon minced garlic
1 jalapeño chile, in chunks with seeds
1 cup plain yogurt
2 tablespoons vegetable oil
1 teaspoon brown sugar
½ teaspoon ground cumin
½ teaspoon paprika
¼ teaspoon turmeric
salt and pepper to taste
4 to 6 boneless chicken breast halves, with skin

At home, combine onion, ginger, garlic, jalapeño, yogurt, oil, brown sugar, cumin, paprika, turmeric, salt, and pepper in blender or food processor. Purée until smooth.

Place chicken in plastic container or large zipper-lock bag. Pour on marinade to coat evenly and seal. Pack in ice chest.

At campsite, prepare grill. Remove chicken, shaking off excess marinade, and grill until opaque and lightly charred, turning frequently. Serve hot.

SERVES 4

MEDITERRANEAN LAMB BROCHETTES

For an upscale Provençal evening around the campfire, don't forget the wine, extra rosemary sprigs for tossing into the fire for added fragrance, and a crusty baguette.

2 tablespoons herbes de Provence
6 garlic cloves, minced
½ cup olive oil
½ cup lemon juice
salt and pepper to taste
8 rib lamb chops, boned and cut into chunks
1 lemon, washed and cut into 8 wedges
1 onion, peeled and cut into 8 wedges
4 plum tomatoes

At home, whisk together the herbes de Provence garlic, olive oil, lemon juice, salt, and pepper. Place the meat in a plastic container or zipper-lock bag, pour on marinade, and seal. Pack in ice chest with skewers.

At campsite, prepare the grill. Make 8 small skewers, alternating lemons, onions, and meat, with a plum tomato in the center of each. Grill, turning frequently to avoid burning, until evenly charred.

SERVES 4

CARNE ASADA

Remember a cutting board and your best camping knife when grilling skirt steak for tacos. Pepper lovers should char a few meaty poblanos to peel and cut into strips for tucking into tacos for additional heat. Beer on ice is the beverage of choice.

1½ pounds skirt steak
½ cup lime or lemon juice
2 onions, cut in ½-inch-thick rings
tortillas
prepared salsas and lime wedges

At home, trim meat of excess fat. Pour lime or lemon juice into large zipper-lock bag, add meat, press out air, and seal. Meat should be evenly coated in juice. Pack in ice chest.

At campsite, build a fire or preheat grill. Grill steaks and onions until evenly charred, just a few minutes per side. Heat tortillas individually on grate or stacked and wrapped in foil.

To make tacos, slice meat into thin strips across the grain. Stuff tortillas with meat and a few onion slices. Serve with salsas and lime wedges.

SERVES 4

GARLIC CHILE STEAKS

There is something about the great outdoors that just calls out for a barbecued steak, corn or potatoes, and ice cold beer.

2 tablespoons chile powder
4 garlic cloves, minced
1 teaspoon cumin
1 teaspoon brown sugar
¼ cup Worcestershire sauce
4 (1-inch thick) New York or shell steaks

At home, combine chile powder, garlic, cumin, sugar, and Worcestershire in small bowl to make a paste. Rub all over steaks and transfer to large zipper-lock bag. Press out air, seal, and pack in ice chest.

At campsite, prepare grill. Grill steaks over hot coals about 5 minutes per side for rare. Serve hot.

SERVES 4

CAMPFIRE QUESADILLAS

Try making these at home, on a stovetop grate, for a rustic lunchtime snack. Tortillas toasted on the grill develop a wonderful earthy aroma. They make a nice small supper, breakfast, or lunch.

6 small corn tortillas
2 cups shredded cheddar or
    mozzarella cheese or mix
1 (7-ounce) can diced roasted green chiles
prepared salsa (optional)

Prepare fire or grill. Over low flame, place tortillas on grate. Cook just 1 minute or 2 to soften, and turn with tongs. Place about ¼ cup cheese in center of each and top each with about a teaspoon of chiles and salsa, if desired. Immediately fold in half to enclose. Press with tongs to seal edges and continue cooking, turning frequently, until cheese melts and edges of tortilla are charred. Serve hot.

SERVES 2 TO 6

CHICKEN AND SHIITAKE PACKETS

Remember to bring the foil for this Chinese meal in a package. Rice, beer, tea bags, and fortune cookies would be nice complements.

2 skinless, boneless chicken breast halves, cut in strips
¼ cup soy sauce
¼ cup dry sherry
2 tablespoons Chinese oyster sauce
2 garlic cloves, minced
4 dried shiitake mushrooms
2 scallions, trimmed

At home, place chicken strips in zipper-lock bag. In small bowl, combine soy, sherry, oyster sauce, and garlic. Pour over chicken and seal bag to marinate. Pack in cooler.

At campsite, boil 1 cup of water and pour over mushrooms in bowl. Let soften 15 minutes. Drain and trim stems.

Start a fire. Make packets with 2 large sheets of foil. Divide chicken and place in center of each sheet. Top each with 2 mushrooms and a scallion. Fold over and seal the edges well. Cook on the coals or over indirect heat on a covered grill about 10 minutes, turning once. Check chicken for doneness and serve over rice.

SERVES 2

WHITEFISH AND FENNEL PACKETS

Licorice-scented fennel and lemons are typical Mediterranean flavorings for fish.

mild whitefish fillets such as
   red snapper or sole
salt and pepper
thinly sliced fennel
fennel leaves
thin lemon slices
lemon juice
herbes de Provence
olive oil (optional) for drizzling

Have ready one large sheet of foil per serving. Season fillets (one per serving) all over with salt and pepper. Start a fire or grill.

Layer each sheet with a few fennel slices, a fish fillet, and two lemon slices. Sprinkle with a few drops of lemon juice, herbes de Provence, and oil, if desired. Fold over to wrap well and seal packets. Place directly over warm coals or on covered grill over indirect flame. Cook, seam-side up, until fish is done, about 10 minutes.

SERVES 2 TO 4

ODDS, ENDS,
AND
DESSERTS

CAMPFIRE BAKED APPLES

*The inspiration for these campsite apples
came from the chef at one of Los Angeles'
best-known Italian restaurants.*

tart apples such as Granny Smith
brown sugar or "Sweet Spice Mix (see page 23)

With a small, sharp knife, remove apple cores.
Fill with a spoon or two of brown sugar. Wrap
in foil and bury in warm, ash-covered coals.
Bake about 20 minutes, until soft. Serve with
spoons.

S'MORES

Just in case you are one of the rare Americans without a taste memory of the traditional Girl and Boy Scout dessert treat, here are toasted-marshmallow chocolate bar sandwiches à la graham. If time is of the essence, start out with chocolate-covered grahams, or if it is variety you are after, try slathering the crackers with strawberry jelly and then coating with chocolate. Yummm!

6 graham crackers, broken in half
6 small, thin milk chocolate bars
12 marshmallows

Around the campfire, top each
graham cracker half with half a bar of
chocolate to cover. Toast the marshmallows on a long stick. Place 2 marshmallows
over 6 chocolate-covered crackers and close
with another chocolate-covered cracker, pressing to melt the chocolate and make a gooey,
sticky marshmallow sandwich.

MAKES 6 SANDWICHES

HIGH-ENERGY
PEANUT BUTTER BALLS

These are so good and easy to put together, you may find yourself keeping a stock in the refrigerator at home for emergency afternoon energy boosts.

⅔ cup chunky peanut butter
⅔ cup flaked coconut
2 tablespoons dry milk
2 tablespoons semisweet chocolate chips
coconut for dipping

Mix peanut butter, coconut, dry
milk, and chocolate chips together in
bowl. Break off tablespoon-size chunks
and roll between palms to form balls. Place a
handful of additional coconut in small bowl.
Dip and roll each ball to coat evenly. Place on
tray in freezer to set, ½ hour. Transfer to
zipper-lock bags and store in refrigerator or
ice chest.

MAKES 10

CAMPFIRE BAKED PEACHES

freestone peaches
whole roasted almonds
honey, maple syrup, brown sugar, or "Sweet
  Spice Mix" (see page 23)

Halve the peaches and remove pits. Dip almonds in honey or maple syrup and place one in center of each half. (If using brown sugar or spice mix, sprinkle center with a spoonful.) Close with second peach half and wrap in foil to enclose. Bury in warm, ash-covered coals. Bake about 20 minutes, until peaches soften. Serve with spoons.

To Toast Bread

Special grates are available at camping stores for making toast on a camp stove. If you don't want to invest in one of these, you can improvise with a grate placed over the burner set to a low flame. Or you can toast bread in a hot, dry skillet (spread a little bit of butter on the bread first).

OAT BERRY BARS

These easy bar cookies are a play on granola bars. Much better than the store-bought kind, they are also messier and should be individually wrapped to travel well.

1½ cups rolled oats
1 cup all-purpose flour
¾ cup brown sugar
½ teaspoon baking soda
½ teaspoon salt
1 stick plus 6 tablespoons butter, melted
1 cup dried cranberries or sour cherries
1 tablespoon grated orange zest
½ cup semisweet chocolate chips

Preheat oven to 350 degrees F.
Line a 9-inch-square baking pan with
parchment paper.

In a large bowl, combine oats, flour, sugar,
baking soda, and salt. Pour in butter and stir
to moisten evenly. Stir in cranberries, zest, and
chips. Press into prepared pan and bake 40
minutes, until edges begin to brown. Cool in
pan and cut into squares. Wrap each in foil.

MAKES 24

Spice Mixes and Rubs

Personalized spice mixes are a handy addition to the home or camping pantry. When you don't have time to marinate, just rub into the item to be grilled and let sit 20 minutes or so for the flavors to sink in. Save and wash out old spice bottles and lids or purchase tiny Tupperware containers for transporting. Be sure to label the containers so you know just what you are blithely sprinkling all over the place.

MEXICAN SPICE MIX

Great for chicken, beef, or any meat.

2 teaspoons coarse salt
2 teaspoons black pepper
2 teaspoons dried crushed oregano
1 teaspoon ground cumin
½ teaspoon ground coriander
¼ teaspoon cayenne
1 teaspoon onion powder

Mix all ingredients in small bowl. Store in small zipper-lock bag or spice container.

CAJUN SPICE MIX

1 tablespoon coarse salt
1 tablespoon white pepper
2 teaspoons cayenne
1 teaspoon black pepper
2 teaspoons paprika
1½ teaspoons garlic powder
1½ teaspoons onion powder
½ teaspoon dried sage
2 bay leaves, crushed

Mix all ingredients in small bowl. Store in small zipper-lock bag or spice container.

NIGHTFALL BAKED POTATOES

*A great, substantial way to greet the day—
smoky baked potatoes with plenty of butter and
the trimmings of your choice.*

Idaho potatoes
butter, sour cream, bacon bits,
    grated cheddar cheese
salt and pepper

After dinner, scrub potatoes clean and wrap
each in foil. Bury in hot coals. In the morning, unwrap and serve for breakfast with
butter, sour cream, bacon bits, and cheddar
cheese. Season to taste with salt and pepper.

CONVERSIONS

LIQUID

    1 Tbsp = 15 ml
    1/2 cup = 4 fl oz = 125 ml
    1 cup = 8 fl oz = 250 ml

DRY

    1/4 cup = 4 Tbsp = 2 oz = 60 g
    1 cup = 1/2 pound = 8 oz = 250 g

FLOUR

    1/2 cup = 60 g
    1 cup = 4 oz = 125 g

TEMPERATURE

    400° F = 200° C = gas mark 6
    375° F = 190° C = gas mark 5
    350° F = 175° C = gas mark 4

MISCELLANEOUS

    2 Tbsp butter = 1 oz = 30 g
    1 inch = 2.5 cm
    all-purpose flour = plain flour
    baking soda = bicarbonate of soda
    brown sugar = demerara sugar
    confectioners' sugar = icing sugar
    heavy cream = double cream
    molasses = black treacle
    raisins = sultanas
    rolled oats = oat flakes
    semisweet chocolate = plain chocolate
    sugar = caster sugar